CLEAVAGE

CLEAVAGE

Chris Tysh

ROOF BOOKS
NEW YORK

ISBN ISBN: 1-931824-13-4
Library of Congress Catalog Card Number 2004096477

Cover art, "Cleavage" by Elizabeth Murray
Cover photo by George Tysh

Grateful acknowledgment is made to the editors of the magazines in
which these poems first appeared: *Aufgabe*, *Chicago Review*, *Dispatch
Detroit*, *Fence*, *gender[f]*, *Hambone*, *Jacket*, *Mirage*, *New American
Writing*, *No: A Journal of the Arts*, *PomPom*, *Skanky Possum*, and
Talisman.

The author wishes to thank Wayne State University for a Summer
Research Grant and The Humanities Center for an Innovative
Projects Grant which provided precious time during which portions
of this book were completed. Additional support was provided, in
part, by a Fellowship from the National Endowment for the Arts.
Special thanks to Ted Pearson for his help with manuscript prepara-
tion and layout.

Roof Books are distributed by
Small Press Distribution
1341 Seventh Avenue
Berkeley, CA. 94710-1403.
Phone orders: 800-869-7553
www.spdbooks.org

 This book was made possible, in part, with public funds
from the New York State Council on the Arts,
NYSCA a state agency.

ROOF BOOKS
are published by
Segue Foundation
303 East 8th Street
New York, NY 10009
segue.org

for Nancy Jones, *de tout mon cœur*

CONTENTS

'ruined invisibly by the silence that cleaves language'
Maurice Blanchot

A as in Annie, ante builder

How do I start?

The photograph would go here
endless leg moving risers right
up to the part where he cries
her name in his sleep

Barbary figs. Pre-war prick
a tinge of peach by virtue of
tide tables on the upper floors

"You're gonna sit on it
all day or what?"

She's running down the street *comme une folle*
little stucco tits out in the open
it'd have to be a red light staggering
patois up the Boulevard as if the night
crew on strike will not stop punching

ii.

I meant to write
"clock in" out of habit

    and lift her overhead
    like chaste *port de bras*
    a little basket of sentinels
    she stuffs with pink satin chemise

        "Hoo-ha!"

    The avant-garde has the hots
    for a pompom girl
    in the place of depression
    between her breasts an aperçu
    of history flags all
    black with banderoles
    stitched every which way

iii.

You are the alpha of all flash
diction violet and pink
around their ears

If I allow that
        we made a circuit didn't we
        meta foyer
        three-chambered text
        wet nothings
                is right

Go to your room slum shack
slip those on next to your pumps
nerves set on edge covered in white
blossoms the old Olds ruins

transition
about risk

in the short life of *les femmes*
Rag's Burning and away we sail
sirens' apprentices over torch lake

Brigitte, beside herself

Suppose the language of demi-mots
and innuendos—nasty little dickies—plunges
below the belt

She was at work filming the abandoned gardens of Rome when
her water broke

        you'll find him in bed hung like a shelf
        a case of vertigo pooling at his feet

        given adjacency the bar lays out
        its belvedere season
        absolving pronouns from the well

        sweeten your breath for
        the diva spills out her limo
        a string of stagehands sewn
        inside her harem pants

ii.

Three men in a boat like a knee play
for a larger work inch up to shore
their lines lifted off an old almanac
whole scene plastered more queer you die

"Who rang your number, Missy?"

She scales her own gums
having dreamt the long fake
teeth in the feral graveyard

misbehave get zero for conduct
miss junky by a heart and pass out
entrance exams' high walls

I see the gap in your face
push my oar in

iii.

I'm planning to de-metaphorize femininity's plunging neckline
post a guard ready to dive into gorge at the merest ooh-la-la

     "Where's my arc of triumph?"

     Voice lessons will be had. Fear not
     the nodule under skin unbidden mirage
     cutting a hole in the road

     At the orgasm seminar we card everyone
     apparently not all that
     it's cracked up to be
     miraculous ring look-alike halo of saints

Celine, in the custody of

The thing is not to explain the bed
series sharply up nor the modal music
of everyday flesh which opens late
like a tennis court I go to by the lake

        Think torque and bite your lip
        between slut and stag there's enough
        powder for three more lines

        I used to be but now I am

        phantom limbs rephrase my song
        rumor has its brutish tempo
        wants my blood

ii.

I have always suspected her of being a courier
for the narrative camp

        After the beach lost its sex appeal like a ladder
        to a sub-floor propped by melancholy
        something about transparency as a mode of entering
        the stories has me running from the circular saw
        in your head

an argument with naked skillets tiny black marks on the ceiling

        plays the wild card the one of straws and camels
        the one of memory and ruins between her fingers
        martyred cigarette crashes to the deck
        hula-hoop skirt goes next ballet slippers lace
        top in no particular order

iii.

She came to me in my sleep as if she'd just stepped out of a fitting
glistening recognition of the phantasmatic weather I labor under

> One always imagines linking verbs will return
> our gaze retrace our steps to the striped awning
> cabana of that first summer

Celine knows better, *pas vrai*

Désirée, from the depths

What slips from her hand while the metro goes black
is anyone's guess
it's funny how grief outstrips the mirror box sempiternal
coke squeezing her eyes shut

Released on its own recognizance more possessive
than ever the sentence stops in mid-air: crummy details
of her detention already lost in my mouth

a mourning I wear on my ankle like a prayer wheel
I turn and turn until I reach her cell

       Give me your lips. Hand drawn out like a sewing
       pattern I touch yours on either side of the plexiglas

       "Visiting hours are over"

ii.

Wouldn't the bleak account ring a bell
in advance of the telling

                              bleach the fabric
down to skeletal form underneath never far from death

in the silence of these words?

iii.

What I took for signs of possession evades the truth
pieced together measure by measure like a film score
where the music swells the lead's desire to make a scene

the very hatchet job he was hired for

       Eyes closed you bank the fire in quotation
       marks the way I say I to hear myself speak
       while the world racks up its malice points

       even so before long our bodies will have scribbled
       their chickenshit demands on tiny pads
       shot to hell our last chance at ransom

Eva, 11:00 PM

Sooner or later the whole stratagem behind the book
of seductions goes up in flames

               opaque gallicism at my throat
               abc without funds

        Within the province of improprieties Eva stands out
        top-shelf liquor no silicone
        on the grounds that the alarm goes off
        never mind when she makes her deposits

        at the rim of the first circle a bodyguard murmurs
        his preference for blondes in that fearsome tongue
        one confesses murder or a tempest in a teapot
        will testify to some tenderness below her breasts

Is it possible to read the passion according to
every chapter and verse and still be in the dark

stash of nylons in the attic not a single metal clip
to tie the thing together

ii.

I mandate the vernacular out!
       evicted from my chambers

please take off your robe

iii.

Lying on her belly she welcomes the brick
concession sure that the building
fever will ease her sleep disorder

to reach the dormitory behind iron curtain
write your own critique scalding remark
goes up an octave

      hand on hip the collective clings
      to its version memorized in obedience

      let off the hook you swing by
      the regulars at the window
      take the edge off with a word or two

Fanny, at the finish line

In the event that my romance with American
idiom turns *idée fixe* a hang-up one sees
from the solarium you will pull me aside
—I who am the "other woman"—

standing next to disaster in a string bikini
        and send me packing

sleepless crows darken the island

       That which is yet to dent
       her conviction not even a tooth mark
       showing has already folded its wings

"Give us a puff, luv"

       such is the empire of doubt now boarding

ii.

I invent a frame where mother and child
exit a bakery

> ruinous shred like a Torah
> scroll I hit upon
> mother nibbles *un baba au rhum*
> medium heels stateless passport
> she consents to her pariah status

> lowest of all and haunted by the root

iii.

Looking at it now padded shoulders
red cinch belt I recognize her first words
inconsolable encounter with jouissance
skin hollow port

                    a pack of wolves the better to
                    defect at crack of dawn

a lovely go-for-broke melody reverses its chorus
little bunny foo foo hopping through the forest

Gigi, night goalie

They think her simple in a chain that goes
wet behind the ears blood graffiti
positioning the self for a penalty kick

Pascal's bet throws its deep shadow over the reeds

I want to suggest an errant text that levels the field
a briefcase at each end no more monkey in the middle
torn panties under pitch meetings

suited and drowsy boys drive
their point past the nub
arched arms domed belly

not the ghost of a chance to score

ii.

We pick the perp in a line of stress
evenly spaced throughout the page

      like a beast abjection works us
      nonstop one day couldn't
      be bothered the next

      although peripheral to the heart
      which weighs on me like a panel
      truck rounding the corner on three wheels

iii.

     Meanwhile Gigi drank her sports metaphors
     in big gulps two balls per mouthful
     like a good girl or social construct

               nearly busted

     a box explodes a chair leaves
     no need to baby-sit more analogies
     sex takes care of writing it up for the zine

You come and go each night like a metal curtain at lockup
deep teen song rearranged by the ways of the hood pockets
inside out

Hannah, handcuffed

I'll whistle the secret letters of discontent
stretch your palindromic arms to either jamb
knowing anguish wears my zigzag tiara to bed

      Reproach me not   Here's a cinéma-
      vérité moment with salad fork and garter-
      belt narrating a game of snitches

      who fingered whom in the last resort

      skittish anatomy of betrayal or banal
      threshold one enjambs for credit

      cherchez la femme, mes amis

ii.

Since she can never be defined (*weib mujer donna*) an empty sign
floats around these bones we take for proof and tie the knot where
a vague torment battens down the hatches

       grigri writing exhaust our murderous lines

       veil with black crepe all mirrors

           "Please everyone I know what I'm doing"

       20 stitches

as if nothing
ripped or blown

Ivy, idiomatically speaking

I might walk in her shoes spiked
with wild cherries tattooed on a box

      ahead of the curve I swerve
                serpentine voices like famine
      in the pestilential river shot in super 8

every summer the subject matter returns
like a punishing fantasy or fragment sentence that hangs
me up with its bad history prying the lid
                off the upper class

      a girl's life drops its shiny cover
      onto hot asphalt
      golden goose for the little
      Judases that we are

ii.

OK so we sold her down the river
who's to say just mourners wear
their faces long

                      tell your *salades*
               to others not born yesterday

a lull in the surf, her body's darker home
white Casbah its own cage awakes
to insolent text, vast patch of lies

evening dalliance with fear scrubs us clean

iii.

Had I studied the theory
of colonial gaze soaking through
thin silk, pale arms cleaved
to the absent material of their lives

        veiled & hemmed in patrimony

        I'd be lining up my ducks
        scattered feathers plump those
        airy pillows pinch a seam
        before they burst in boiling water

iv.

lower than low
in a small *cinéma de quartier*
so long ago

really a peephole
to siphon off my quota

later under varsity sky you jump
a barricade blast hole
in sweatshop rhetoric

tiny speck of blood
for pigs in the audience
credits roll like heads
sous la terreur

Justine or *la joie de vivre*

of milky beds
      yellow tea rose
           foothold for soft belly boat

                    one could do worse than
                    eat out of your wet palm

or bang the magazine brass
sorry story scooped (& schtupped)
already slipping from its column

    dogs' midnight racket

    some are carried away on a stretcher color of sienna
    retaining walls which read
                "Eat the rich!"
      marquis' castle sags in its middle
               creeping jennie
      and crab apple everywhere

ii.

Clip-clop horsy
succumb to my venom

        once a whore always . . .
        stenciled Sadean letters
        worn down to doughnut holes

        such a prophecy it was
        sweet cinnamon buns wrested
        from vending machine

They used to call it fair
sex maybe a tart
apology by the skeleton
crew as if nothing
trashy jarred this nightly plant

iii.

Risen

      on the shore of your girlhood

      like Nausicaa washing her

linen

      arrive, child

      the ramparts are in shambles

      let them tie a can to their whatchamacallit

         suffice to loosen

         the dead's grip on us

         leech effect done with

            ploughed under

               obsolete beach

Kate's karma

Thought to have fainted
"swooned," she wrote in high school Brit
when I saw my name on the pass sheet

      minuscule white placard
      amid gray bricks

Same scandal veils
present war with forgetting

         "This is not a hotel, ma"

Arms heavy buckets
hardly a trope for daughterly love
nor cheap gloss on suffering

         "Come on, get some sleep now"

ii.

You'd suck blood
so long as I hung
on your coattails

dirty sum we repay
in small excrements
prickly pears of consent

time to rewrite
the whole maternal bed
and its flimflam cargo

remember that ancient cleft
place where "you go your way
                    I go mine"

barren immemorial debt from before "before"

                    What shape do I give it now
                    hair brush rattle chair be there
                    on the morrow

                    kyrie eleison

iii.

phantom silhouette

playing hard to get

(fate) fixing the odds

red over black for now

Laure my love

Help me out here.
It could have been the year of the painted bird or maybe before
when Dirty vomits at the Savoy.
I'm getting all mixed up.
There's a war, barracks desert-like.
We don't hear the screams not even rain that pounds still less
the dark blood running down their legs.
Maybe I'm thinking of the sisters in *Les Années de Plomb*.
Bomb fetish.
A close-up in a cell, synchrony, recurrent yeast infection.
She misspells whiskey.
The postponement of forgiveness.
Slack prejudice.
Fuzzy sweaters.
Should the worst storm—heap of eyeglasses silver bangles—
turn up the volume
we pore over the omen.
You're toast.
I'm shagging you on all fours. Put that corset. *Y a du monde au balcon*
no more common than my thumb on your pulse.

Mira mid-sentence

like she meant to murder

charred bits of food stuck on tongue

those impossible foreign names

the path of breath breaks

over

skis

ditch

yawn

double diphthongs in a row

(life) could you be any more alien

Mademoiselle Dobiecki

minding her onions

falls behind her Latin

a lifeless lump, unfashion'd, and unfram'd.

ii.

Incapable to adhere to blond hair
flat chest narrative's noble shield
I fold one girl onto another
                    spoon fashion

                    gradually pronouns
                    unroll their mats
                    puckered lips whisper
                                "My name is not . . ."
                    in transient summer night

Outside seamless gutters
shoes in hand I squat
caught in the muddy
romance of pulp

                    hang my head
                    like a droopy peony
                    before the wire pulls me up
                    from the green orphanage

iii.

On the road to transparency
what is there muslin thin
from debris to debris

        our kind living it up
        in mock opulence

        "Your papers, please"

        I see your belly button
        grow sorrel, crooks of elbows
        harbor plans to blow

        this colony on the outskirts of good manners

        the rest of the verses sung sotto voce
        as if a lullaby en route to the precinct
        threading through noon traffic

Nadja, no man's island

It is said

        the black continent's nomad desire
        drives it mad like the bald-headed
        woman who walks all the way from
        Laos to the Ganges shore selling
        her twelve children as she goes

Beyond my strength

        under these conditions to arrange
        for another rendezvous
        all but asterisked words
        roughly strewn on gravel

        blindfold and gangbang facts
        gutted
                postscript
                      at the door
"I am the soul in limbo"

ii.

Even if hatless
        bare legs running up debts
        these tulip glasses won't explain
        the nakedness of left bank
            overlapping screams
                in the lobby

So much for the geography of chance
        a salt block dear André
        licks before each swallow

Convulsive or not, N's life presses through
        her eyes like a sieve
        gold bullion
            not served at the Claridge

        Strange that
            homeless men come near her

"Excuse me, Madame, I've lost my compass"

            as birds with St. Francis
        strip her tongue
            for parts
            .

iii.

Flanked by men in white
she returns to the very street
of self-abandon

derelict candle here and now
before the sky in "risky" turns ultraviolet red
let's cart this leaky fable of hope
                              надежда indeed

I say indoor plumbing weekly rates
that is the sublime rebuff she's after

                    nocturnal

                    muffled

                    demand

to recast the passage
                    about fork in the road
                    crude shroud
                              is the dress of chance

                    black foment in her hair

O, obbligato

hole of the chain

bent over

stone floor

bound

law

in the half-light

of consent

ii.

I confess I've erased the voice
that accompanies this performance
frozen on the old frame

50 years hence a gang of girls
waits to pounce on me as if text

        were flesh
        sexual fix holding a pose
        —crow tree downward facing dog—
        prone to S/M hanky codes:
        blue on top red under green means harder

to whip this script into mutuality
        leather lulus, novice all
learning to switch and shout

        "Cat got your tongue?"

fling your curse
      clip chains & pegs
           into the erotic oubliettes

their cutting ends
        nothing more than traces
        of the prisoner's endless night

Phoebe and the phantoms

Contrary to the light
        held in her name
        bowed phaeton now idle

a shadow hangs all over the place
        paternal plot that goes
        for the teeth under the axe
        of time

                notched forward like tiny pleats
                nid-d'abeilles—shirred work done in chain
                stitch—"I heard it through the grapevine"
                and " Your daddy's rich"

Make a hissing sound
        at the frontier

butter in your mouth
        will not spill the letters
                piled high
                      on sibilant white plain

ii.

To flood

the engine

in my lap

die-hard

untenable suspense

shrouded

oriflamme

so-called paradise

dance

running counter

"Phoebes, you're next"

iii.

Unable to sleep, shuffle
     deck of phantasms
     think limbs
     sent flying over chin-up bar

Couched in black mesh,
     chest open to the sky
     the fall and rise implies a dream
     riverboat lanterns
          now that
     we man the traffic (of) signs
     redeem old ghosts

          o carcass
          o shadow

          done in

          grassy redress
     for the unforgiving math
          (of need)

Queenie quarantined: a sonnet

Remember
Querelle that
incomparable dance sequence
the sailor's boat neck
maillot only the languid music
of Brest formed with the front
of the tongue touching the hard place
barred from intercourse with the shore marked vessel
goes back among saffron waters to nurse hunger they
serve with narrow hips skin like a child drawing a
face on fogged up glass pleading to stay his demons "Whoa!"
the hardy orchids trouble the senses why paper over these twists of
fate rip out old sidewalk when concrete figures bright assenting voice pours in
strings mordant and ravenous the harbor dive only a first drop of the serum

Reiko, r for riddle

A silent letter left unopened
        is always a matter of meter
running out no more support

from here on high no more
        campaign to expose imaginary
register of this encounter, poor

draft register impasse, the girl
        in a red tank top leather mules
sums up her station without words

sums up the dirty bush of verities
        lacquer finish track lights flick on
"*Sumimasen*, how could you?"

ii.

My first was covered in dew
        fluted pink, step in cave
or roof of mouth the other way

around increases gravity's mouthpiece
        the bit that passes for marks
that mirror tall girl in train station I'd have

said something consoling like you still have
        a chance it's not too late
to make that work—you don't know the half of it—

the very thought of it might hit the ceiling
        impenetrable lump cake knot
stone rock bone clotted dream, please

the only one I count on will not please
        nor beg off his turn at the switch
not that I'd have the nerve to ask

iii.

As far as the eye can see
        she's gone blond for miles
underground lair sleeveless and suggestive

dresses hang in the closet as if suggesting
        old forms could walk past their masters
rewrite own lines into tiny installments of rebirths

at the *samsāra* gate the line wends its way like a slug
        resist temptation to round your back
as you enter do not tear or cleave clean the heart

of the slim story whose heart rhymes with struggle
        her body so transparent so light with self
a mossy plank you'll walk on again and again, helpless

Sonia, something liquid or sheer

Unbound from any narrative pact
stranger in parentheses
without allegiance, curtains of intent
I move the trash like chestnuts from a fire
first one leg then soft humus underfoot
Bite me! Say hello to the rat hole! Screw up
your courage little centauress there's too many straws
to seize too many puffs on the gloomy square
accent falls on mimesis, social space made to echo
the rumpus, heavy wagons come to a head monstrous
pay-off for the abduction of souls
sentenced to the black book

ii.

At dawn the cats are out
what's to stop us now that a head
of light has tangled sheets just missed
wires in the palace
let's read Vladimir Ilich Ulyanov straight through
I'll roll each "R" as if me Yuri you Lara
thread the needle through fog
it's a fact without qualities same as ever
we conspire—do not be deceived
by white hands doll face—
to blow our brains before the train
enters suddenly white with snow

iii.

O the sumptuous con of writing!
fish with golden fins sky-high
banquet the singing bard and more
how easy to install partisans on the river
about to storm this red and white detachment
come on, Sonia, the dream was pretty clear
all were fed except for me
there's a little girl at that moment of the story
who cries like a gull or screaming muni bird
"Give me some" but it's too dark now to shoot
Go on, you'll find him in the attic
the unmentionable, you see, hasn't happened yet

Tristessa, to trace after

All gifts
rise up
in a spoon

inscrutable
doorway
of hags

a thought apart
from the heart
incarnate

even where
mournful
holy mother

gives a hand
to the thief
beats it home

the one burning
glance the other
stone blind

ii.

they say
steal the thunder
like this

ellipsis, all
that passes
in the air

withers away
so long my bride
my drunken boat

pegged and scored
like a screen
to a window

that inaugural mirage
behind your eyelids
that soft sugar halo

just enough to die
in one's shoes
or stand by

iii.

Were it my duty
to review grievous cupola
oddly waffled

like a Chinese coat
I'd do it in shifts
night after night

the book slides
from its headboard
black signs on brown

maidenly skin
and savage intelligence
I roll across the bed

water stones and all
cascade down her bodice
carrying off the eyes

Umang, unfolding

for Michal Rovner

(her) story falls
               dead
               through the cracks

snow or ash
               the girls walk in pairs
               deaf man's hand squeezing

               words from
                    thin air

under a *clair de lune*
          yellow apron in the sky
               boils down to cinnamon
bark

          play ball
               or
                    whack someone

ii.

Wait!
      Could it be we
            who are blind
            lead the killers

to the body

            blue sari asleep
in the raw splendor
      of before
            the strip
            search
                lapses

into nighttime torch
            or just after
            crescent moon
doubts it can reach
            a bargain

iii.

That the war inlays

      shadow

      to oily sheen

     unshaven cotton headgear

       goes without saying

   here are signs

         tracking dirt

   along the other's hem

       in vain

girls whip

      the shredded wash

       by hand

in vain

    sift

       river's lies

iv.

while in the bonbon room we write

       stretch

          versions

             for the record

       spindly pack of bacchantes that we aren't

war's memory wire

          uncut

Viv's *vague à l'âme*

For every melancholy absence of the real
I substitute
        seedy simulacrum clatch of malcontents

           blowing smoke up their ass
           "ta-da!"
switch words

           on her dance card
           in that faint
                  thin-blooded scrawl

the muezzin dawn has a fondness for
        you will have recognized beat up
                motorcycle jacket black slip she

           wears as if in a dream matrix
              here a hint
                of softness in the straw

pulls back what one's allowed
              to see: cleavage's
        pharmakon word
(cure and poison)   on the rim

ii.

the very form of writing
made flesh
                    wire bed cotton

batting
            lodged under false pretense
I teeter

                    then play a movement
passionaria—scorch of gas and face masks—
            "Silence! *On tourne*"

            hoisted so one may ring the change
or fall back on ropes' default status
                    the future anterior of the wounded world

further press into the body
                    of work
                            —entrenched idea

            like a thick wallet or factory building—
            red and black filaments
            upon water cannons
            bloody lineations on white sheets

iii.

Who said "I will not mix
        contexts?"
                the feeling that

        evidentiary status of war
        continues
                to sweep the room

like spilled hooch
                        "I have a leg
        in the cooler"

                this *tête du fémur*
        conceals a migratory story
from Barbie foot to juvie hall

        as if sleepwalking, women
                return to the bar
                        involuntary angels

        each deposition irresistible keystrokes
        tell nothing but
                long spokes
        (of flesh)   in the cross-hairs

Wei, wordlessly

Either way the object will be constructed
In relation to others: snow piano factory
Or rice paper written into the estate
Of longing as if to denote we have words
For such steamy kinship; sheet music too
Frayed by now her pink kimono sleeves
A vantage point on the icy bridge I take
Her name to mean "rose" or "precious"
Either way nothing forced oblivion's lodger
To go about like a ghost, "will be my death"
She who wrote only from the heart that
Fabled letter of the river-merchant's wife
Call it risky matter of deferral like difference
That spans the abyss between speaking and writing
Either way eating at all that marks and signs his name

ii.

Little remains of beginner's mind
Unless you count low-frequencies
All lapses erasures and dead air
After the quake, hearing returns
Dizzy *Waltz for Debbie* unseen sally
Of green linnets in eardrums
As if to rejoin from other side
"Come, come" the defense bench
Little inversion she practiced while
The case went out the door
Which is not the end she sleeps on
Inside tent city a blue-haired lookout
Will never be sure of being still enough
To parse motley aviary snarled down below
Little remains of sounds like slugs or surf on brain

iii.

Then nothing. Silence. Sleeping
Pill or tapeworm will absorb writing
Fled from the chamber of self-expression
Fix's in, confession's out upon this floor
Of dry ice among us or else case study
For resurrecting the idea Marx's red mole
Has a way to transport us like an elevator shaft
Up and up the heave and rip of time from infancy
Then nothing to buy with all these silkworms
These busy little cocoons spelling a different
Story still to come for lack of dying words
Turned inside out the Chinese dancers' skirts
Become parachutes, advance signs in the *clair-obscur* sky
Then nothing more save a flare, flickering letters against earth

iv.

To each
Her own
Ripple
Going
Places
It would
Not
Kill you
To remember
A Hundred
Flowers
Sold to the
Blind
Young bride
To each a sign

Xenie, exaggeratedly pale

Should you know the book
       where words grow black
       tufts of reeds scribbled palm

           "No it's not Death
           It's only poor little Xenie"

I'll step closer in
       to have it out with nudity
       fever scimitars no doubt
       clasping the fleshy rounds

each one more exquisite
       than un *cœur à la crème*
       found crushed around the stem
       as good as all things swear

    for themselves that vigil's burden
    makes plain what love conceals
    from the hard bed

ii.

That accent—graven—on the blank
       space of her chart

       could be dark bruises
       small diacritic marks
       like a set of tinctures
             seeping through

       the one that blushes incognito
             tears away
       her gaze transparent face passing
             for nursemaid

             "It's about time"

             "Fess up"

who held the tar of essence
who went to market
             the smooth pelt we call self

iii.

No necromancy on my watch
    no skanky snake oil
        can
            remove the redundant
               passage of death

            "Not the kid"

    none will drink from
        le petit lait
      that sets in

      sweet surrender
to figurality's run for cover

      how very pale
    your breasts are
          neither vestal nor vixen

I nuzzle their snow
      tie up the fly legs
      before we all go down

Yvonne's yes-no eyes

Only yesterday things followed the curved nail of doubt back to camp

with its own cast like father and son so green bough to main branch

private largesse documents our station stacked up against a wall

we exhaust self-portraiture in the face of lesser faults deadpan stare

isn't it too late to shoulder your way past the crowd skilled at havoc

if what they're after deepens the hole the more one thinks the night

grainy film like soot calls up a truce "I can breathe now" like Orpheus

emerging from underground we revive the high beam we have been

allowed to read by unless this cause a problem scooping the urn

furry with moss obvious pulse racing now to spit hair yank stump

ii.

Better off not to hoard a certain corpus vulnerable avatar

though it may be of everything "feminine" rousing itself

from its scare quotes bras and panties like so many grunts

punching holes miles from home as if a barker could usher in

the one and only perfect ten campfire girl now sawn in half

"ladies and gentlemen" see how many places you can sharpen

the bit as long as she who descends never mentions having eaten

from amnesia's plate tarnished diadem drifting down her back

by way of analogy with wax doll meant to evoke the rosy

ready-made palpability of sex "mama don't cry"

iii.

Pick a letter she'd said from a to z the very gamut promises

an open form you'll find a round of dandelion or lightning

bolt made of ice atop a cloud I'm afraid I might have used

these words more than once it's possible several poems

already noted such inadequacy between parts like turning

the floor to children let us oblige the notion that cleavage

is not an ark and what we sense as singular nursery room

legend a mere click of the repressed "what do you think

you're looking at?" when the river whips the leaf dragon

and the girl is sent to bed without her dinner bun

Zoe, a zone of her own

head and neck
torn loose
from the mortar

of your class
what mirror
image lives on

nonchalance's
twin sister
and funny bone

what tends to
fill the racks
speculum

won't wrinkle
the skirt
still it's done

FLASHES

our sex
on the
program

you are handed
a sentence
in the language

of nuts
and bolts as if
wearing

a tool
apron "hush"
someone's whistling

a tune about a tumble
in a castle
on whom to

R I V E T

a fallen shadow
such hymns
in the collection

box do us tender
pain
"don't touch"

there goes the pattern
of repetition even birds
comprehend

here a fiction
builds a face
out of

B R A C K E N

its black ends
touching
like a stack

of chairs
not for nothing
were you cited

for using
wrong key
on your mind

if misty faeries
did indeed
watch over

said cradle
I'll borrow
a sugar cup

and learn
to walk
on the cusp

of invention
gliding onto wrought
iron

H A N D R A I L

like a lock
that is shot
or Kafka's gymnast—

it doesn't
matter which—
basket

you pack
with
similes

ii.

our desire to be drilled about the interior
—elaborate hanging baroque cloth—lays bare
her waist   unwanted practice
of looking behind   she records

into the mix laughing head off now back to the wall
instead of me lecher   daughter   unnameable
rivers and mountains pass each evening as if watching
them stream   from a balustrade

later situationists we think it best to abolish all
remembrance   of origin
roots like corpses   a dialogue of mutes
"excuse me, where you're from?"

if words are lit these girls women present company
included then writing's promise is a   bombshell
hear the hissing serpents I've plucked from our head
mark the dream of the three   sirens

iii.

not because ill   or in deep doubt   over

exit   clanking one's way   toward

   farewell indolence   a shaft of light   after

the porch party   moves indoor   no one dares

        to blink   let alone

clasp and split   as if   o yesterday

      were a pocket   I adumbrate   roughly

zone by zone   enunciate   the whole

     dress particular   for such occasion

    even the skeptics   trade in their gear

        for a sliver   of skin

going   off the roof   in the wee hours

wedged in   behind   patience's fern

          the template   locates all

twenty-six   desires   buttonholes

          parts of speech   as palimpsest

to spring through   tangle   of letters and castings

     if there be blood   a road map   I could ever

decipher   lottery ticket   or coup d'état   blow

     a fireball   after the dolls   *au petit bonheur*

la chance   salt their wounds   as you would

     a radish   undeterred   "put that

in your tablets"   like a paper   cutout   the vigil

          over   burned   mouth

turns out   delirious   dialogue

     we alone   translate   as masks

iv.

Pre-war prick, between her breasts, we made a circuit
Having dreamt the feral graveyard, halo of saints
Phantom limbs, everyday flesh will return to narrative camp
Crummy details I took for signs in quotation marks
Behind iron curtain, you made a scene in a fearsome tongue
Standing next to disaster, sleepless crows darken the island
A chain that goes wet like a panel truck or metal curtain at lockup
Who fingered whom battens down the hatches, wears tiara to bed
I'll scrub the golden goose; siphon off her quota under varsity sky
One could do worse than succumb to my venom; arrive child
Flimflam cargo; "You go your way I go mine" on the morrow
Should the worst storm, put that corset help me out here
I fold one girl onto another on the road to transparency
It is said life presses through, nocturnal dress of chance
In the half-light that accompanies this endless text, leather lulus all
Teeth under the axe, so-called paradise dance next
Barred from glass, rip out old sidewalk touching the hard place
Roof of mouth, something consoling at the *samsāra* gate
Say hello to stranger in parentheses to echo the rumpus
Inscrutable glance, holy mother gives a hand to the thief
Snow or ash, we write river's lies
For every melancholy a dream matrix on her dance card
As if scrawled like a ghost into the estate of longing
"No, it's not Death," figurality's run for cover
A certain corpus calls up analogy with wax doll, yes-no eyes
Torn loose from the mortar of your class, still it's done

Glossary of Foreign Words and Phrases

A¹   *comme une folle*: like a crazy woman

A²   *port de bras*: carriage of the arms; a ballet term used to describe a movement of the upper torso and arms; in the Russian method there are six port de bras

A³   *les femmes*: the women; also as in the women of the French M.L.F. (women's liberation movement)

C³   *pas vrai*: isn't that right?

F¹   *un baba au rhum*: a French sponge-cake steeped in rum syrup

H¹   *cherchez la femme, mes amis*: look for the woman, my friends

H²   *weib mujer donna*: German, Spanish, Italian words for "woman"

I²   *salades*: in the metaphorical sense, untrustworthy stories, lies

I⁴   *cinéma de quartier*: neighborhood movie theatre

—   *sous la terreur*: literally, under the terror, a reference to The Reign of Terror (1793–1794) of the French Revolution characterized by a wave of executions of presumed enemies of the state

J¹   *la joie de vivre*: the joy of living

K²   *kyrie eleison*: Greek for "Lord, have mercy!" an expression used in Christian liturgies, although it antedates Christian worship

L¹   *Les Années de Plomb*: (English title: Marianne and Juliane), 1981 film by Margharete von Trotta

—   *y a du monde au balcon*: French colloquial expression to denote large chest; she's a buxom one

N³   *надежда*: Russian word for hope

P¹   *nid d'abeilles*: decorative stitching that uses shirring, often found on baby clothes in France

Ω_   *querelle*: French word for quarrel; a direct reference to Rainer Werner Fassbinder's 1983 movie, *Querelle*, based on a text by Jean Genet

R¹   *sumimasen*: Japanese for "excuse me"

R³   *samsāra*: from Sanskrit, the cycle of existences and rebirths

U¹   *clair de lune*: moonlight

V¹   *vague à l'âme*: French expression to denote a sentiment of sadness without a discernable cause; melancholy or dreamy state

—   *pharmakon*: the Greek word translating to "medicine" but meaning both cure and poison, used by Plato in Phaedrus and by Jacques Derrida as deconstructionist play in his essay, "Plato's Pharmacy"

V²   *passionara*: Spanish for an impassioned one; a fervent female militant who defends a political cause, sometimes in a violent and spectacular way

—   *On tourne*: movie director's command, "we're shooting"

V³   *tête du fémur*: top of the thigh bone

W³   *clair-obscur*: French for chiaroscuro, the interplay of light and shadow

X¹   *un cœur à la crème*: dessert made with cream cheese in a heart-shaped mold

X³   *le petit lait*: literally, little milk, used in a familiar expression as in lap it up

Z³   *au petit bonheur la chance*: at random; to do something in a happy-go-lucky manner; hit or miss

ROOF BOOKS

- ❏ Andrews, Bruce. **EX WHY ZEE**. 112p. $10.95.
- ❏ Andrews, Bruce. **Getting Ready To Have Been Frightened**. 116p. $7.50.
- ❏ Benson, Steve. **Blue Book**. Copub. with The Figures. 250p. $12.50
- ❏ Bernstein, Charles. **Islets/Irritations**. 112p. $9.95.
- ❏ Bernstein, Charles (editor). **The Politics of Poetic Form**. 246p. $12.95; cloth $21.95.
- ❏ Brossard, Nicole. **Picture Theory**. 188p. $11.95.
- ❏ Cadiot, Olivier. **Former, Future, Fugitive**. Translated by Cole Swensen. 166p. $13.95.
- ❏ Champion, Miles. **Three Bell Zero**. 72p. $10.95.
- ❏ Child, Abigail. **Scatter Matrix**. 79p. $9.95.
- ❏ Davies, Alan. **Active 24 Hours**. 100p. $5.
- ❏ Davies, Alan. **Signage**. 184p. $11.
- ❏ Davies, Alan. **Rave**. 64p. $7.95.
- ❏ Day, Jean. **A Young Recruit**. 58p. $6.
- ❏ Di Palma, Ray. **Motion of the Cypher**. 112p. $10.95.
- ❏ Di Palma, Ray. **Raik**. 100p. $9.95.
- ❏ Doris, Stacy. **Kildare**. 104p. $9.95.
- ❏ Dreyer, Lynne. **The White Museum**. 80p. $6.
- ❏ Edwards, Ken. **Good Science**. 80p. $9.95.
- ❏ Eigner, Larry. **Areas Lights Heights**. 182p. $12, $22 (cloth).
- ❏ Gizzi, Michael. **Continental Harmonies**. 92p. $8.95.
- ❏ Goldman, Judith. **Vocoder**. 96p. $11.95.
- ❏ Gottlieb, Michael. **Ninety-Six Tears**. 88p. $5.
- ❏ Gottlieb, Michael. **Gorgeous Plunge**. 96p. $11.95.
- ❏ Gottlieb, Michael. **Lost & Found**. 80p. $11.95.
- ❏ Greenwald, Ted. **Jumping the Line**. 120p. $12.95.
- ❏ Grenier, Robert. **A Day at the Beach**. 80p. $6.
- ❏ Grosman, Ernesto. **The XULReader: An Anthology of Argentine Poetry (1981–1996)**. 167p. $14.95.
- ❏ Guest, Barbara. **Dürer in the Window, Reflexions on Art**. Book design by Richard Tuttle. Four color throughout. 80p. $24.95.
- ❏ Hills, Henry. **Making Money**. 72p. $7.50. VHS videotape $24.95. Book & tape $29.95.
- ❏ Huang Yunte. **SHI: A Radical Reading of Chinese Poetry**. 76p. $9.95
- ❏ Hunt, Erica. **Local History**. 80 p. $9.95.
- ❏ Kuszai, Joel (editor) **poetics@**, 192 p. $13.95.
- ❏ Inman, P. **Criss Cross**. 64 p. $7.95.
- ❏ Inman, P. **Red Shift**. 64p. $6.
- ❏ Lazer, Hank. **Doublespace**. 192 p. $12.
- ❏ Lazer, Hank. **Doublespace**. 192 p. $12.
- ❏ Levy, Andrew. **Paper Head Last Lyrics**. 112 p. $11.95.

- Mac Low, Jackson. **Representative Works: 1938–1985**. 360p. $12.95, $18.95 (cloth).
- Mac Low, Jackson. **Twenties**. 112p. $8.95.
- McMorris, Mark. **The Café at Light**. 112p. $12.95.
- Moriarty, Laura. **Rondeaux**. 107p. $8.
- Neilson, Melanie. **Civil Noir**. 96p. $8.95.
- Osman, Jena. **An Essay in Asterisks**. 12p. $12.95.
- Pearson, Ted. **Planetary Gear**. 72p. $8.95.
- Perelman, Bob. **Virtual Reality**. 80p. $9.95.
- Perelman, Bob. **The Future of Memory**. 120p. $14.95.
- Piombino, Nick, **The Boundary of Blur**. 128p. $13.95.
- Raworth, Tom. **Clean & Will-Lit**. 106p. $10.95.
- Robinson, Kit. **Balance Sheet**. 112p. $11.95.
- Robinson, Kit. **Democracy Boulevard**. 104p. $9.95.
- Robinson, Kit. **Ice Cubes**. 96p. $6.
- Scalapino, Leslie. **Objects in the Terrifying Tense Longing from Taking Place**. 88p. $9.95.
- Seaton, Peter. **The Son Master**. 64p. $5.
- Sherry, James. **Popular Fiction**. 84p. $6.
- Silliman, Ron. **The New Sentence**. 200p. $10.
- Silliman, Ron. **N/O**. 112p. $10.95.
- Smith, Rod. **Music or Honesty**. 96p. $12.95
- Smith, Rod. **Protective Immediacy**. 96p. $9.95
- Stefans, Brian Kim. **Free Space Comix**. 96p. $9.95
- Tarkos, Christophe. **Ma Langue est Poétique—Selected Works**. 96p. $12.95.
- Templeton, Fiona. **Cells of Release**. 128p. with photographs. $13.95.
- Templeton, Fiona. **YOU—The City**. 150p. $11.95.
- Torres, Edwin. **The All-Union Day of the Shock Worker**. 112 p. $10.95.
- Ward, Diane. **Human Ceiling**. 80p. $8.95.
- Ward, Diane. **Relation**. 64p. $7.50.
- Watson, Craig. **Free Will**. 80p. $9.95.
- Watten, Barrett. **Progress**. 122p. $7.50.
- Weiner, Hannah. **We Speak Silent**. 76 p. $9.95
- Wolsak, Lissa. **Pen Chants**. 80p. $9.95.
- Yasusada, Araki. **Doubled Flowering: From the Notebooks of Araki Yasusada**. 272p. $14.95.

ROOF BOOKS
are published by
Segue Foundation, 300 Bowery, New York, NY 10012
Visit our website at **segue.org**

ROOF BOOKS are distributed by
SMALL PRESS DISTRIBUTION
1341 Seventh Avenue, Berkeley, CA. 94710-1403.
Phone orders: 800-869-7553
spdbooks.org